The Wisdom of the
PARABLES

The Wisdom of the PARABLES

Robin Langley Sommer

Barnes & Noble Books
NEW YORK

CRITICAL: decorative border ornaments

Page 1: *Christ with the cross, by Michelangelo.*

Page 2: *A medieval sheepfold, from a Book of Hours, recalls Christ the shepherd's flock.*

Page 3: *A detail from Michelangelo's frescoed ceiling of the Sistine Chapel:* The Creation of Adam *(1508–12). Psalm 104 is one of many that celebrate God's acts of creation.*

This edition published by Barnes and Noble, Inc., by arrangement with Saraband Inc.

Copyright © 1998 Saraband Inc.

Design © Ziga Design
Editor: Robin Langley Sommer

Library of Congress Cataloging in Publication Data available

ISBN: 0-7607-0793-6

Printed in China

10 9 8 7 6 5 4 3 2 1

Acknowledgements
Extracts from the Authorized Version of the Bible (The King James Bible), the rights in which are vested in the Crown, are reproduced by permission of the Crown's Patentee, Cambridge University Press.

The publisher would like to thank the following people for their assistance in the preparation of this book: Nicola Gillies, art editor; and Wendy J. Ciaccia, graphic designer. Grateful acknowledgement is also made for the illustrations featured in this book, which are reproduced by courtesy of Planet Art and CorelDraw, except those on pages 14, 15, 30, 41, 43, 51, 52, 53, 66 and 77, which are courtesy of Saraband Image Library.

This book is dedicated to the Reverend Canon Leonard A. Cragg

CONTENTS

On Vocation

On Spirituality

On Doorways Open and Shut

Index of Parables

INTRODUCTION

The word "parable," derived from the Greek *parabolé* (comparison), describes a brief allegorical story that conveys a moral lesson, spiritual principle, or universal truth. There was a long tradition of parabolic teaching in the East when Christ undertook His teaching ministry, but the stories He told have lived for 2,000 years. At the heart of them are everyday events like a woman searching for a lost coin, a farmer concerned about the weeds in his grain field and a father welcoming his son home. But underlying their apparent simplicity is a power that conveys truth to anyone who seeks it, because these tales were told by Christ and bear the unmistakable stamp of His personality and of the radical message He brought. As Scripture scholar C.W.F. Smith observed in *The Jesus of the Parables* (1948): "[Here] Jesus appears as no Eastern sage or objective moralist, but as the Initiator of God's new age and the Agent of His purpose. He is not [only] the kindly advocate of brotherly love, but the revealer of the dreadful love of God and the awe of the divine mercy."

Christ drew upon the rabbinic parables when he told the stories that left an indelible impression upon people's minds. The Evangelists wrote that "the people were astonished at His doctrine; for He taught as one having authority, and not as the scribes" (Mt 7:28–29). Luke tells us that He spent three days in the Temple at the age of twelve, "sitting in the midst of the doctors, both hearing them, and asking them questions. And all that heard him were astonished at his understanding and answers" (2: 46–47).

The parables of Christ added a new dimension to the oral and written tradition of the Hebrews. One aspect of it was a deep empathy with the natural world, as seen in the parables of the Mustard Seed, the Budding Fig Tree, the Lost Sheep, the Lilies of the Field and many others. Throughout the Gospels Christ expressed a love for the animal creation that was unparalleled in antiquity. His teachings are filled with images from nature that show compassion for all creatures and intuitive knowledge of their ways. Animals are often used as images of spirituality as contrasted with worldliness. When Christ mourned over Jerusalem, He compared Himself to a hen that wanted to shelter her chicks under her wings to protect them from danger (Mt 23:37). He saw the shepherd, the sower and the vinedresser as people in touch with God through their affinity with the natural world.

Christ also showed profound insight into the best (and worst) in human nature. He taught that every person had equal value in the eyes of God and must be treated accordingly. His bias was toward the poor and afflicted, whom the world considered no one, but His invitation was to all. The many parables of grace and of the Kingdom call for human effort and co-operation, but their primary emphasis is on the loving initiative of God in establishing divine order in all relationships. The parables of the Good Samaritan, the Prodigal Son and the Good Shepherd pushed far beyond the boundaries previously set by every religion between God and humankind. Christ was the first to call God "Father." This concept was radically new, unheard of until His coming. It shifted the whole basis of morality from crude human ideas of justice to the immeasurable mercy of God as manifested in Christ. To this day, the parables serve as an open door to those who first asked 2,000 years ago: "We should like to see Jesus" (Jn 12:21).

ON FAITH

〜〰〰〜

On Faith

Previous page: A Renaissance painting by Bellini shows Christ transfigured between the prophets Moses and Elijah before His wondering disciples.

Among the best-known parables on faith are those of the Hidden Treasure and the Pearl of Great Price. They may have been told together, or grouped together later, as parallelism is characteristic of Hebrew style. Other examples of twin parables include the Mustard Seed and the Leaven and the Houses Built on Sand and on Rock.

The theme common to the Hidden Treasure and the Pearl of Great Price is the joy of attainment. In the first parable, the treasure is found by accident—perhaps buried for safekeeping by a wealthy person in time of war. The fortunate man who comes upon it while he is digging sells all that he has to buy the field and make the treasure his own. The merchant, on the other hand, has spent his life buying and selling pearls. He knows their worth, and is vigilant about finding the peerless pearl. When he does so, he invests all he has to acquire the pearl of great price. In his case, the finding of the pearl is the result of long and deliberate seeking, but both he and the farmer, whose find far exceeded his hopes, achieve the same gifts of grace.

The importance of a sound foundation is expressed in the parallel of the Two Builders. Christ draws a contrast between hearing and then acting according to His teachings, and hearing without taking action. The man who builds his house on a stone foundation will not be swept away when temptations and trials assault him, but the person who builds upon sand—perhaps in one of the *wadis* subject to periodic flooding in the Middle East—will see his house collapse. This example of the difference between hearing and doing has an antecedent in the Book of Proverbs (10:25), which reads: "When the whirlwind passeth, the wicked is no more: But the righteous is an everlasting foundation."

The parable of the Mustard Seed speaks to the concepts of enlargement and shelter through faith, while that of the Leaven emphasizes the idea of transformation. The tiny size of the "grain of mustard"—metaphorically, the initial act of faith—is contrasted with that of the mature "tree" (actually a large bush, some eight to ten feet tall), which offers shelter to the birds that alight on its branches. Like its counterpart, the parable of the small amount of leaven or yeast that can activate a great mass of dough, this parable foresees the extension and growth from small beginnings of the Kingdom, which offers both shelter and nourishment to all who are drawn to it, including the Gentiles.

The twin parables of the Patch and the Wineskins have sometimes been interpreted as a statement of incompatibility between Judaism and Christianity. However, this ignores the fact that Christ repeatedly stated that he had come to complete the Old Law, not to abolish it. It was an axiom that patching an old garment with new (unshrunk) cloth would only make the tear worse. Likewise, everyone knew that new wine poured into old wineskins would burst them. What is implied here may not be incompatibility, but a creative synthesis, such as that made explicit in Matthew's parable of the householder whose treasure is of greater value because it consists of both new and old elements (13:52). It is possible that these three stories were told together but transcribed separately.

One of the many beautiful parables from nature is that of the Sower, whose seed stands for the teaching that will yield an abundant harvest for the Kingdom of God. At the same time, the seed represents the listeners, who must undergo a process of growth and maturation. Each of those who first heard this parable could identify with the adversities faced by the sower— marauding birds, scorching sun, careless people treading

Below: *The farmer, as depicted here by Van Gogh, figures in many of the Gospel parables, which were addressed mainly to the country people of Israel.*

down the seedlings, weeds springing up. Each new problem called for a hopeful response based on the conviction that the harvest was certain despite human frailties, because God's purpose could not be thwarted. This parable combines realistic warnings about the difficulties faced in pursuing the life of the spirit with encouragement that failures and trials can be instrumental to spiritual growth, and that faith through adversity brings deeper spiritual values.

In the Unjust Judge, we find a parable of grace that contrasts the behavior of the unjust judge with that of God. The judge is defined as a hard-hearted, corrupt official who "cared nothing for God or man." The only reason he finally gives in to the widow's pleas for justice is that she has worn him out. His behavior is not to be admired; rather, he seeks his own self-interest even in doing the right thing. All through the Bible, the widow represents those who need aid and compassion. Here she stands for everyone who asks for help urgently in prayer, and unlike the judge, God is moved by her urgency and responds in kind. The lesson of this parable is "how much more" God will hear the prayers of His people and do them justice.

According to Matthew, the parable of the Sheep and the Goats was the last one spoken by Christ before His passion and death. It looks forward to the end of time and prophesies His second coming in glory to reward the just and segregate those who still have to learn the meaning of mercy. The contrast between the sheep at the king's right hand— a symbol of divine favor and authority—and the goats, whose false pride has distanced them from God and others, is a stark one. Neither "saints" nor "sinners" are fully aware that their compassion, or lack of it, is the criterion whereby they have, in fact, judged themselves. But Christ makes this unmistakably clear when he says, "Inasmuch as ye have done it unto one of the least of these my brethren, ye have done it unto me." Thus Christ proclaims both His solidarity with all people through the Incarnation and the fulfillment of the new law of love in His person. This teaching has been variously described as: the Mystical Body of Christ, encompassing all creation; the Shekinah, or manifestation of Divine Presence; and the Great Spirit, source and sustainer of all that is. The message is clear, no matter how one defines it. Unconditional love and compassion draw us closer to God as we understand God.

Grace is the theme of the parable often called the Importunate Friend. Like the unjust judge, the drowsy householder first refuses his neighbor's urgent request, not because of ill will, but because it is inconvenient for him to get up and answer the door. However, the neighbor's persistence carries the day. He throws himself upon the mercy of his friend quite shamelessly, pressing his request for three loaves of bread to feed the hungry visitor who has arrived unexpectedly in the middle of the night. He makes no pretense of being a good neighbor, a good host or a good anything. His need is his only claim on the sleepy householder, who finally gets up and gives him what he asks for. This parable speaks to our utter reliance upon the mercy rather than the justice of God, to grace as a gift offered freely to all rather than a merit badge handed out to a select few for observing all the rules.

Below: The afflicted Christ on the Way of the Cross, from a medieval Book of Hours.

THE HIDDEN TREASURE AND THE PEARL OF GREAT PRICE

44 Again, the kingdom of heaven is like unto treasure hid in a field; the which when a man hath found, he hideth, and for joy thereof goeth and selleth all that he hath, and buyeth that field.

45 Again, the kingdom of heaven is like unto a merchant man, seeking goodly pearls:

46 Who, when he had found one pearl of great price, went and sold all that he had, and bought it.

—MATTHEW 13:44–46

Below: The house unwisely built on a poor foundation collapses in the storms of adversity: "and the ruin of that house was great."

HOUSES BUILT ON ROCK AND SAND

47 Whosoever cometh to me, and heareth my sayings, and doeth them, I will shew you to whom he is like:

48 He is like a man which built an house, and digged deep, and laid the foundation on a rock: and when the flood arose, the stream beat vehemently upon that house, and could not shake it: for it was founded upon a rock.

49 But he that heareth, and doeth not, is like a man that without a foundation built an house upon the earth; against which the stream did beat vehemently, and immediately it fell; and the ruin of that house was great.

—LUKE 6:47–49

THE MUSTARD SEED AND THE LEAVEN

31 Another parable put he forth unto them, saying, The kingdom of heaven is like to a grain of mustard seed, which a man took, and sowed in his field:

32 Which indeed is the least of all seeds: but when it is grown, it is the greatest among herbs, and becometh a tree, so that the birds of the air come and lodge in the branches thereof.

33 Another parable spake he unto them; The kingdom of heaven is like unto leaven, which a woman took, and hid in three measures of meal, till the whole was leavened.

—MATTHEW 13:31–33

Left: *A woman kneads bread dough containing the leaven (yeast) that will make it rise into a wholesome loaf.*

New Cloth on Old Garments; New Wine in Old Bottles

Below: A pastoral scene by Van Gogh recalls the homely wisdom contained in this parable of contrasts between the Old Law and the New.

36 And he spake also a parable unto them; No man putteth a piece of a new garment upon an old; if otherwise, then both the new maketh a rent, and the piece that was *taken* out of the new agreeth not with the old.

37 And no man putteth new wine into old bottles; else the new wine will burst the bottles, and be spilled, and the bottles shall perish.

38 But new wine must be put into new bottles; and both are preserved.

—LUKE 5:36–38

THE SOWER

1 And he began again to teach by the sea side: and there was gathered unto him a great multitude, so that he entered into a ship, and sat in the sea; and the whole multitude was by the sea on the land.

2 And he taught them many things by parables, and said unto them in his doctrine,

3 Hearken; Behold, there went out a sower to sow:

4 And it came to pass, as he sowed, some fell by the way side, and the fowls of the air came and devoured it up.

5 And some fell on stony ground, where it had not much earth; and immediately it sprang up, because it had no depth of earth:

6 But when the sun was up, it was scorched; and because it had no root, it withered away.

7 And some fell among thorns, and the thorns grew up, and choked it, and it yielded no fruit.

8 And other fell on good ground, and did yield fruit that sprang up and increased; and brought forth, some thirty, and some sixty, and some an hundred.

9 And he said unto them, He that hath ears to hear, let him hear.

10 And when he was alone, they that were about him with the twelve asked of him the parable.

11 And he said unto them, Unto you it is given to know the mystery of the kingdom of God: but unto them that are without, all *these* things are done in parables:

12 That seeing they may see, and not perceive; and hearing they may hear, and not understand; lest at any time they should be converted, and *their* sins should be forgiven them.

13 And he said unto them, Know ye not this parable? and how then will ye know all parables?

14 The sower soweth the word.

15 And these are they by the way side, where the word is sown; but when they have heard, Satan cometh imme-

diately, and taketh away the word that was sown in their hearts.

16 And these are they likewise which are sown on stony ground; who, when they have heard the word, immediately receive it with gladness;

17 And have no root in themselves, and so endure but for a time: afterward, when affliction or persecution ariseth for the word's sake, immediately they are offended.

18 And these are they which are sown among thorns; such as hear the word,

Below: The diligent sower who has overcome all the dangers that threatened his crop is rewarded by a bountiful harvest.

19 And the cares of this world, and the deceitfulness of riches, and the lusts of other things entering in, choke the word, and it becometh unfruitful.

20 And these are they which are sown on good ground; such as hear the word, and receive *it*, and bring forth fruit, some thirtyfold, some sixty, and some an hundred.

—MARK 4:1–20

THE UNJUST JUDGE

1 And he spake a parable unto them *to this end*, that men ought always to pray, and not to faint;

2 Saying, There was in a city a judge, which feared not God, neither regarded man:

3 And there was a widow in that city; and she came unto him, saying, Avenge me of mine adversary.

4 And he would not for a while: but afterward he said within himself, Though I fear not God, nor regard man;

5 Yet because this widow troubleth me, I will avenge her, lest by her continual coming she weary me.

6 And the Lord said, Hear what the unjust judge saith.

7 And shall not God avenge his own elect, which cry day and night unto him, though he bear long with them?

8 I tell you that he will avenge them speedily. Nevertheless when the Son of man cometh, shall he find faith on the earth?

—LUKE 18:1–8

Below: The first to show faith in the "Son of Man" were those present at the Nativity: Mary and Joseph, the herald angels, and the shepherds and Wise Men.

THE SHEEP AND THE GOATS

31 When the Son of man shall come in his glory, and all the holy angels with him, then shall he sit upon the throne of his glory:

32 And before him shall be gathered all nations: and he shall separate them one from another, as a shepherd divideth *his* sheep from the goats:

33 And he shall set the sheep on his right hand, but the goats on the left.

34 Then shall the King say unto them on his right hand, Come, ye blessed of my Father, inherit the kingdom prepared for you from the foundation of the world:

35 For I was an hungred, and ye gave me meat: I was thirsty, and ye gave me drink: I was a stranger, and ye took me in:

36 Naked, and ye clothed me: I was sick, and ye visited me: I was in prison, and ye came unto me.

37 Then shall the righteous answer him, saying, Lord, when saw we thee an hungred, and fed *thee*? or thirsty, and gave *thee* drink?

38 When saw we thee a stranger, and took *thee* in? or naked, and clothed *thee*?

39 Or when saw we thee sick, or in prison, and came unto thee?

40 And the King shall answer and say unto them, Verily I say unto you, Inasmuch as ye have done *it* unto one of the least of these my brethren, ye have done *it* unto me.

41 Then shall he say also unto them on the left hand, Depart from me, ye cursed, into everlasting fire, prepared for the devil and his angels:

42 For I was an hungred, and ye gave me no meat: I was thirsty, and ye gave me no drink:

43 I was a stranger, and ye took me not in: naked, and ye clothed me not: sick, and in prison, and ye visited me not.

44 Then shall they also answer him, saying, Lord, when saw we thee an hungred, or athirst, or a stranger, or naked,

or sick, or in prison, and did not minister unto thee?

45 Then shall he answer them, saying, Verily I say unto you, Inasmuch as ye did *it* not to one of the least of these, ye did *it* not to me.

46 And these shall go away into everlasting punishment: but the righteous into life eternal.

—MATTHEW 25:31–46

Left: *The awe-inspiring vision of the Last Judgement, featuring the Risen Christ, painted by Michelangelo for the Sistine Chapel during the 1530s.*

THE IMPORTUNATE FRIEND

5   And he said unto them, Which of you shall have a friend, and shall go unto him at midnight, and say unto him, Friend, lend me three loaves;

6   For a friend of mine in his journey is come to me, and I have nothing to set before him?

7   And he from within shall answer and say, Trouble me not: the door is now shut, and my children are with me in bed; I cannot rise and give thee.

8   I say unto you, Though he will not rise and give him, because he is his friend, yet because of his importunity he will rise and give him as many as he needeth.

—LUKE 11:5–8

Right: Rembrandt's Head of Christ *(1650) is a moving portrait of the teller of this parable that encourages perseverance in prayer. Conversely, Christ is also "the importunate friend" who seeks to awaken us to our spiritual identity as children of God.*

ON
RELATIONSHIPS

On Relationships

Previous page:
Gustave Doré's
nineteenth-century
engraving of Christ
teaching in the Temple.

All of the parables on relationships described here have two levels of meaning, based on the new model of Christ as exemplar of both the fully human and the divine. They show that it is the humble and the outcasts who are most receptive to His teachings on grace as against judgement, in relationships with God and with one another.

In the story of the Two Sons whose father asks them to work in the vineyard, the first refuses to go, and the second answers with a facile "Yes, sir," but does not obey. Meanwhile, the first son realizes that he has offended his father by his refusal and changes his mind. In the end, it is he who goes into the vineyard to do a day's work. Christ compares the two brothers to those who responded to John the Baptist's call for repentance and those who ignored it, respectively. He tells his hearers that "the publicans [the despised Roman tax collectors] and the harlots believed him: and ye, when ye had seen it, repented not afterward, that ye might believe him."

This parable is analogous to that of the Pharisee and the Publican, usually cited as an example of humility commended by Christ versus smug self-righteousness. Both these men were at prayer, the Pharisee giving thanks that he wasn't sinful like the tax collector over there (the Publican) who, in turn, was "standing afar off" with downcast eyes praying, "God be merciful to me a sinner." In fact, *neither* of them has a legitimate claim on God's grace, but the Publican knows it, while the Pharisee is still picking through the rummage bag of his supposed good works to justify himself. As theologian Robert Farrar Capon puts it in his provocative book *The Parables of Grace* (Eerdmans, 1988): "We all long to establish our identity by seeing ourselves as approved in other people's eyes." Therefore, he continues, we concern ourselves with appearances rather than true values, and we are consequently afraid of exposure. However, we cannot hide our true natures from God, and we should work to build loving relationships instead of distancing ourselves through false barriers.

Another well-known parable is that of the Good Samaritan, who goes out of his way to help a Jewish man assaulted by robbers and left for dead. There had been intense antipathy between the Jews and the Samaritans on religious grounds since the conquest and repopulation of Samaria, part of Israel's Northern Kingdom, by Assyria in 721 BC. Thus, the Biblical command to "Love thy neighbour as thyself" (Lev. 19:18) was not construed by Christ's audience as extending to the Samaritans. The Jews sought to limit the definition of "neighbour" to fellow members of their faith community. Christ turned this idea on its head by showing the lengths to which the Samaritan went in rescuing the unfortunate wounded man, who had been ignored by both a priest and a Levite. In fact, he risked his own life by lifting the injured man onto his beast of burden to carry him to the next town. The seventeen-mile road between Jerusalem and Jericho was a haunt of bandits, where violence was so frequent that historian Josephus called this route "the Ascent of Blood." In this parable, Christ preaches a revolutionary doctrine of unbounded compassion flowing from each person's inestimable value in the eyes of God. The touchstone of this unique value for the Christian is the fact that Christ died for all on the "ascent of blood" to Calvary.

The universal offer of salvation recurs in the parable of the Wedding Feast, a retelling of a traditional

Below: Originally an expression of abhorrence, "Samaritan" came to represent Christian charity and goodwill through the teachings of Jesus. Here, Christ amazes the Samaritan woman at the well by asking her for a drink of water.

rabbinic parable. The king who prepared a feast for his son's marriage first invited those who could be considered fit to attend, but all of them made excuses and refused the invitation. Angered, he told his servants to invite new guests, so they "gathered together all as many as they found, both bad and good: and the wedding was furnished with guests." The king approved all who had come except for a single guest who did not have on a clean garment (symbolic of repentance). He was excluded from the feast, as in the original version found in the Babylonian Talmud, which concludes: "Let those who have adorned themselves for the feast sit and eat and drink; but as for those who have not adorned themselves…, they shall stand and look on."

One of the most telling parables on relationships is the story of the Unmerciful Servant. He owed his master an immense debt—10,000 talents (a quantity of gold or silver)—and was about to be sold into slavery with his whole family when he begged for mercy and promised to pay all that he owed. His master "was moved with compassion and loosed him, and forgave him the debt." But rather than follow his master's example, the unmerciful servant went out to a fellow servant who owed him a small sum, seized him and throttled him, demanding, "Pay me that thou owest." Ignoring the debtor's pleas for patience, the unmerciful servant had him thrown into prison. When their master heard of it, he was extremely angry and had the hard-hearted servant punished severely. Lest anyone should miss the point of this story, Christ made it explicit: "So likewise shall my heavenly Father do also unto you, if ye from your hearts forgive not every one his brother their trespasses."

The parable of the Lost Sheep has touched human hearts for almost 2,000 years. Here the tragedy of desolation—of being cut off from one's community—is redressed by a seeking God, in the person of the shepherd, who will not rest until he has found the strayed member of his flock. Sheep are highly social animals, and one that has strayed is nearly helpless unless it can attach itself to a familiar human being. For this reason, the shepherd has to carry the bewildered animal back to the flock "on his shoulders." The emphasis on the joy of the shepherd and his friends over the recovery of the lost sheep reflects the "joy [that] shall be in heaven over one sinner that repenteth, more than over ninety and nine just persons, which need no repentance."

This theme deepens in the parable of the Prodigal Son, who left his family after demanding his inheritance "and took his journey into a far country, and there wasted his substance in riotous living." Here, instead of a sheep, we have a man, the most social of all animals, and he has strayed not across a hillside, but into a "far country," where he faces famine and destitution. His lostness is devastating, because he feels cut off from both God and his fellow men. At last, he has a change of heart and resolves to go home as a servant, if his father will have him back. But even as he thinks over his plea to be taken in as a servant, "no more worthy to be called thy son," his father sees him approach and hastens out to embrace him, scarcely heeding his apology in his joy to have him back. The whole household is called upon to prepare a feast and celebrate the prodigal's return. When the responsible elder brother comes in from the fields, he is affronted, but his father

Below: Both the lion and the king are emblems of Christ in His majesty and strength, as seen in this medieval illustration from a Book of Hours.

entreats him to join the celebration, "for this thy brother was dead, and is alive again; and was lost, and is found." Perhaps never before had Christ's Jewish audience heard so strong a statement of God's love for them. It echoes in the human heart to this day, making the story of the Prodigal Son one of the best-loved parables of all.

The story of the Two Debtors is another parable of forgiveness, which contrasts with that of the Unmerciful Servant. Each of the Two Debtors was forgiven his debt by a compassionate creditor, but one had owed far more than the other. Christ poses the question, "which of them will love him [the creditor] most?" The Pharisee Simon replies, "I suppose that *he*, to whom he forgave most," and this judgement is approved by Christ. The story implies that love, which is of God, covers a multitude of sins, and forgiveness is one of its signs. The Unmerciful Servant, by contrast, is depicted as a lost soul, because he can neither receive nor give love, while each of the Two Debtors returns love in proportion to the kindness he has received.

Faithfulness to stewardship of God's gifts is the theme of the Wise Steward, whose responsible behavior in his master's absence is compared to that of the servant who proves unfaithful. According to clergyman Edward A. Armstrong, an authority on folklore and author of *The Gospel Parables* (Sheed and Ward, 1967): "It is possible that [this] parable has been coloured by what happened to Nadan in the Story of Ahikar, preserved in many languages and introduced into the *One Thousand and One Nights*. The Aramaic version dates from the fifth century BC. Believing his uncle, the King of Assyria, to be dead, Nadan gathers 'vain and lewd folk' to a feast and strips and whips the men-servants and handmaidens. He is found out and flogged; whereupon he swells up and bursts asunder." This would account for the uncharacteristically violent punishment described in Luke's account—"cut him in sunder"—which is generally attributed to a mistranslation from the Aramaic.

THE TWO SONS

28 But what think ye? A *certain* man had two sons; and he came to the first, and said, Son, go work to day in my vineyard.

29 He answered and said, I will not: but afterward he repented, and went.

30 And he came to the second, and said likewise. And he answered and said, I *go*, sir: and went not.

31 Whether of them twain did the will of *his* father? They say unto him, The first. Jesus saith unto them, Verily I say unto you, That the publicans and the harlots go into the kingdom of God before you.

32 For John came unto you in the way of righteousness, and ye believed him not: but the publicans and the harlots believed him: and ye, when ye had seen *it*, repented not afterward, that ye might believe him.

—MATTHEW 21:28–32

Below: *Ghiberti's Renaissance sculpture of John the Baptist, whom Christ called the greatest of all the prophets. The poor and the outcast heard his message of repentance most clearly and acted upon it.*

THE PHARISEE AND THE PUBLICAN

9 And he spake this parable unto certain which trusted in themselves that they were righteous, and despised others:

10 Two men went up into the temple to pray; the one a Pharisee, and the other a publican.

11 The Pharisee stood and prayed thus with himself, God, I thank thee, that I am not as other men *are*, extortioners, unjust, adulterers, or even as this publican.

Below: The humility of the Publican (left) was more acceptable to God than the self-righteousness of the Pharisee, who prided himself on fulfilling all the prescriptions of the Old Law.

12 I fast twice in the week, I give tithes of all that I possess.

13 And the publican, standing afar off, would not lift up so much as *his* eyes unto heaven, but smote upon his breast, saying, God be merciful to me a sinner.

14 I tell you, this man went down to his house justified *rather* than the other: for every one that exalteth himself shall be abased; and he that humbleth himself shall be exalted.

—LUKE 18:9–14

THE GOOD SAMARITAN

30 And Jesus answering said, A certain *man* went down from Jerusalem to Jericho, and fell among thieves, which stripped him of his raiment, and wounded *him*, and departed, leaving *him* half dead.

31 And by chance there came down a certain priest that way: and when he saw him, he passed by on the other side.

32 And likewise a Levite, when he was at the place, came and looked *on him*, and passed by on the other side.

33 But a certain Samaritan, as he journeyed, came where he was: and when he saw him, he had compassion *on him*,

34 And went to *him*, and bound up his wounds, pouring in oil and wine, and set him on his own beast, and brought him to an inn, and took care of him.

35 And on the morrow when he departed, he took out two pence, and gave *them* to the host, and said unto him, Take care of him; and whatsoever thou spendest more, when I come again, I will repay thee.

36 Which now of these three, thinkest thou, was neighbour unto him that fell among the thieves?

37 And he said, He that shewed mercy on him. Then said Jesus unto him, Go, and do thou likewise.

—LUKE 10:30–37

Below: *In Doré's engraving, the Good Samaritan lifts the wounded traveler from his horse so he can take care of him at a nearby inn. Through this parable, his actions became a byword for selfless compassion.*

The Marriage Feast

Opposite: *The marriage feast is filled up with guests brought in from all over the countryside, "both bad and good," after those who were invited first refused to come. Only the guest who lacks a wedding garment is excluded.*

2 The kingdom of heaven is like unto a certain king, which made a marriage for his son,

3 And sent forth his servants to call them that were bidden to the wedding: and they would not come.

4 Again, he sent forth other servants, saying, Tell them which are bidden, Behold, I have prepared my dinner: my oxen and *my* fatlings *are* killed, and all things *are* ready: come unto the marriage.

5 But they made light of *it*, and went their ways, one to his farm, another to his merchandise:

6 And the remnant took his servants, and entreated *them* spitefully, and slew *them*.

7 But when the king heard *thereof*, he was wroth: and he sent forth his armies, and destroyed those murderers, and burned up their city.

8 Then saith he to his servants, The wedding is ready, but they which were bidden were not worthy.

9 Go ye therefore into the highways, and as many as ye shall find, bid to the marriage.

10 So those servants went out into the highways, and gathered together all as many as they found, both bad and good: and the wedding was furnished with guests.

11 And when the king came in to see the guests, he saw there a man which had not on a wedding garment:

12 And he saith unto him, Friend, how camest thou in hither not having a wedding garment? And he was speechless.

13 Then said the king to the servants, Bind him hand and foot, and take him away, and cast *him* into outer darkness; there shall be weeping and gnashing of teeth.

14 For many are called, but few *are* chosen.

—MATTHEW 22:2–14

The Unmerciful Servant

23 Therefore is the kingdom of heaven likened unto a certain king, which would take account of his servants.

24 And when he had begun to reckon, one was brought unto him, which owed him ten thousand talents.

25 But forasmuch as he had not to pay, his lord commanded him to be sold, and his wife, and children, and all that he had, and payment to be made.

26 The servant therefore fell down, and worshipped him, saying, Lord, have patience with me, and I will pay thee all.

27 Then the lord of that servant was moved with compassion, and loosed him, and forgave him the debt.

28 But the same servant went out, and found one of his fellowservants, which owed him an hundred pence: and he laid hands on him, and took *him* by the throat, saying, Pay me that thou owest.

29 And his fellowservant fell down at his feet, and besought him, saying, Have patience with me, and I will pay thee all.

30 And he would not: but went and cast him into prison, till he should pay the debt.

31 So when his fellowservants saw what was done, they were very sorry, and came and told unto their lord all that was done.

32 Then his lord, after that he had called him, said unto him, O thou wicked servant, I forgave thee all that debt, because thou desiredst me:

33 Shouldest not thou also have had compassion on thy fellowservant, even as I had pity on thee?

34 And his lord was wroth, and delivered him to the tormentors, till he should pay all that was due unto him.

35 So likewise shall my heavenly Father do also unto you, if ye from your hearts forgive not every one his brother their trespasses.

—MATTHEW 18:23–35

THE LOST SHEEP

3 And he spake this parable unto them, saying,

4 What man of you, having an hundred sheep, if he lose one of them, doth not leave the ninety and nine in the wilderness, and go after that which is lost, until he find it?

5 And when he hath found *it*, he layeth *it* on his shoulders, rejoicing.

6 And when he cometh home, he calleth together *his* friends and neighbours, saying unto them, Rejoice with me; for I have found my sheep which was lost.

7 I say unto you, that likewise joy shall be in heaven over one sinner that repenteth, more than over ninety and nine just persons, which need no repentance.

—LUKE 15:3–7

Below: *A medieval artist was inspired by the parable of the Lost Sheep to depict the well-loved story in his own milieu for a Book of Hours.*

THE PRODIGAL SON

11 And he said, A certain man had two sons:

12 And the younger of them said to *his* father, Father, give me the portion of goods that falleth *to me*. And he divided unto them *his* living.

13 And not many days after the younger son gathered all together, and took his journey into a far country, and there wasted his substance with riotous living.

14 And when he had spent all, there arose a mighty famine in that land; and he began to be in want.

15 And he went and joined himself to a citizen of that country; and he sent him into his fields to feed swine.

16 And he would fain have filled his belly with the husks that the swine did eat: and no man gave unto him.

17 And when he came to himself, he said, How many hired servants of my father's have bread enough and to spare, and I perish with hunger!

18 I will arise and go to my father, and will say unto him, Father, I have sinned against heaven, and before thee,

19 And am no more worthy to be called thy son: make me as one of thy hired servants.

20 And he arose, and came to his father. But when he was yet a great way off, his father saw him, and had compassion, and ran, and fell on his neck, and kissed him.

21 And the son said unto him, Father, I have sinned against heaven, and in thy sight, and am no more worthy to be called thy son.

22 But the father said to his servants, Bring forth the best robe, and put *it* on him; and put a ring on his hand, and shoes on *his* feet:

23 And bring hither the fatted calf, and kill *it*; and let us eat, and be merry:

24 For this my son was dead, and is alive again; he was lost, and is found. And they began to be merry.

25 Now his elder son was in the field: and as he came and

drew nigh to the house, he heard musick and dancing.

26 And he called one of the servants, and asked what these things meant.

27 And he said unto him, Thy brother is come; and thy father hath killed the fatted calf, because he hath received him safe and sound.

28 And he was angry, and would not go in: therefore came his father out, and intreated him.

29 And he answering said to *his* father, Lo, these many years do I serve thee, neither transgressed I at any time thy commandment: and yet thou never gavest me a kid, that I might make merry with my friends:

30 But as soon as this thy son was come, which hath devoured thy living with harlots, thou hast killed for him the fatted calf.

31 And he said unto him, Son, thou art ever with me, and all that I have is thine.

32 It was meet that we should make merry, and be glad: for this thy brother was dead, and is alive again; and was lost, and is found.

—LUKE 15:11–32

Left: *The repentant Prodigal Son hopes to be received back into his home as a servant, but his father's joyful welcome will far exceed his expectations.*

THE TWO DEBTORS

41 There was a certain creditor which had two debtors: the one owed five hundred pence, and the other fifty.

42 And when they had nothing to pay, he frankly forgave them both. Tell me therefore, which of them will love him most?

43 Simon answered and said, I suppose that *he*, to whom he forgave most. And he said unto him, Thou hast rightly judged.

—LUKE 7:41–43

THE WISE STEWARD

42 And the Lord said, Who then is that faithful and wise steward, whom *his* lord shall make ruler over his household, to give *them their* portion of meat in due season?

43 Blessed *is* that servant, whom his lord when he cometh shall find so doing.

44 Of a truth I say unto you, that he will make him ruler over all that he hath.

45 But and if that servant say in his heart, My lord delayeth his coming; and shall begin to beat the menservants and maidens, and to eat and drink, and to be drunken;

46 The lord of that servant will come in a day when he looketh not for *him*, and at an hour when he is not aware, and will cut him in sunder, and will appoint him his portion with the unbelievers.

47 And that servant, which knew his lord's will, and prepared not *himself*, neither did according to his will, shall be beaten with many *stripes*.

48 But he that knew not, and did commit things worthy of stripes, shall be beaten with few *stripes*.

—LUKE 12:42–48

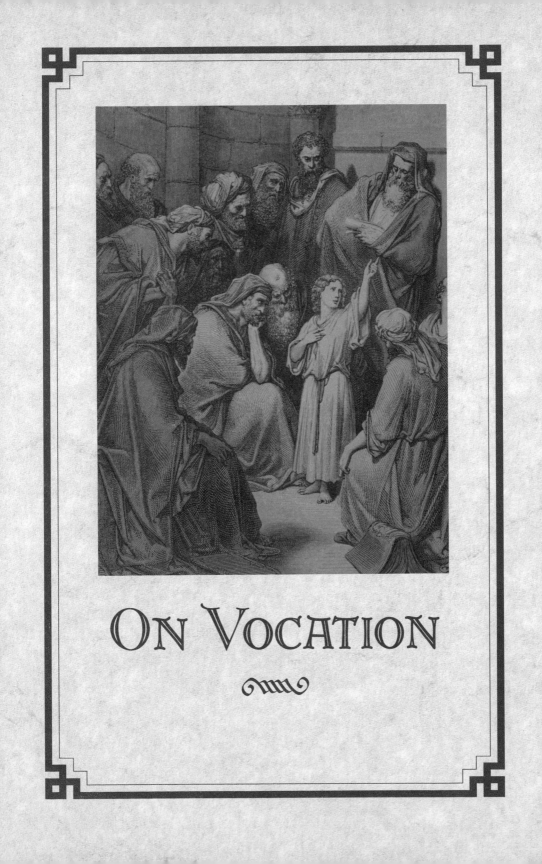

ON VOCATION

ON VOCATION

Previous page:
*Christ's vocation was
first manifested at the
age of twelve, when He
stayed behind His
family in Jerusalem to
learn from the Jewish
elders and to declare
the Scriptures to them.*

The sound of calling reverberates through the New Testament. Christ calls his disciples from their fishing boats to a new vocation as His witnesses; blind Bartimaeus cries out repeatedly for Christ's help, not to be silenced by the crowd; the disciples call Christ from His sleep during the storm on the lake because they are afraid of drowning. In fact, all of the gospels record an ongoing dialogue between Christ and His fellow men and Christ and God, whom He taught them to call "Our Father."

The theme of vocation runs through many of the parables. In the story of the Wheat and the Tares, country people could identify with the plight of the householder who planted "good seed" in his wheat field only to have an enemy come by night and sow weeds among the wheat. The tares are usually identified as a species of rye grass that tastes bitter and causes dizziness if mixed with wheat flour. These weeds were a common problem in the Middle East, and it was impossible to uproot them while the wheat was growing. The householder told his servants to let the weeds grow up with the wheat until harvest time (when the tares would stand erect, while the wheat bent over from the weight of the grain). Then the weeds could be gathered and burnt and the harvest reaped.

Christ explained this parable to his disciples privately as a story of good and evil in life, which would endure until the end of time. Identifying Himself as "the Son of man" [the householder], He explained that "The field is the world; the good seed are the children of the kingdom; but the tares are the children of the wicked one." Only at the last judgement would the two be separated: "Then shall the righteous shine forth as the sun in the kingdom of their Father."

Mercy, rather than strict justice, is the theme of the Workers in the Vineyard. Here, the employer is God, who finds work for everyone in need and pays each enough to buy food for his family, no matter what time of day he began to work. (The "penny" issued to every vinedresser was a drachma or dinarius—the standard payment for a day's work.) Human notions of justice, as expressed by the workers who started earliest, are likely to reflect selfishness and envy. In this parable, Christ urges self-examination and speaks on behalf of the oppressed. Those who came to work latest (the poor) were treated by the employer with far more kindness than the rich would have shown them—and far more than they had expected.

Faithfulness to one's vocation is emphasized in the parable of the Talents, which is about money (abilities) held in trust. Those servants who took risks by trading with their master's money were commended for increasing it, thus showing responsibility. The servant who took no chances, and handed back the sum originally entrusted to him, was berated for burying his talent in the earth. Although the rabbinical law prescribed this as a means of safekeeping, money becomes productive only in circulation, so this servant's narrow sense of responsibility prevented him from taking full advantage of the opportunities offered by active trade. This message would be underscored by St. Paul in his Epistle to the Romans (12:6): "The gifts we possess differ as they are allotted to us by God's grace, and must be exercised accordingly."

The parable of the Unjust Steward has been a puzzle to interpreters from the beginning. Was Christ really commending the steward who told his master's debtors to falsify their records so they could pay less than they

Below: The underlying lesson of the Talents was to make use of God-given advantages. This message would be reiterated through the teachings of St. Paul.

owed? He had just been fired for mismanagement. By his own admission, he conspired with the debtors to avoid becoming a ditchdigger or a beggar. So why did his master praise him as having acted wisely? This parable ends with what has been perceived as an explanation: "for the children of this world are in their generation wiser than the children of light."

Scripture scholar Robert Farrar Capon brings a radically new interpretation to this story in *The Parables of Grace*. In his view, "The unique contribution of this parable to our understanding of Jesus is its insistence that grace cannot come to the world through respectability. Respectability regards only life, success, winning; it will have no truck with the grace that works by death and losing—which is the only kind of grace there is." Pointing out that Christ Himself was considered disreputable by the self-righteous, who conspired to kill Him, he concludes: "This parable...says in story form what Jesus himself said by his life. He was not respectable. He broke the Sabbath. He consorted with crooks. And he died as a criminal. Now at last, in the light of this parable, we see *why* he refused to be respectable: he did it to catch a world that respectability could only terrify and condemn."

There is a strong parallel between the parables of the Lighted Candle and the Body's Lamp (the eye). In the first, Christ's followers are urged to show the light of His mission openly. This had precedent in Hebrew scriptures, where Israel was called the light or lamp of the world. Here, the light is that of Christ Himself.

In the parable of the Body's Lamp, Christ tells his hearers that "when thine eye is single, thy whole body also is full of light." This implies that focusing on Christ and His love—the "one thing necessary" that He commended to Martha, the sister of Lazarus and Mary—will transform one's life.

In the parable of the Rich Fool, Christ warns against the desire for two kinds of wealth: mental and material. First, he tells His disciples to rely entirely upon the Holy Spirit of God when they are threatened by religious or other authorities. They cannot count on well-paid lawyers and well-prepared cases, as others do. Their only security is in their poverty and dependence upon God. Similarly, those who put all their energy into the pursuit of material things are "not rich in God's sight."

Single-mindedness in the cause of discipleship recurs in the twin parables of the Tower Builder and the Warring King. Both challenge Christ's followers to count the cost of their commitment and be ready to persevere despite ridicule, tedium and the very real limitations of their human nature. Self-knowledge and humility are both necessary: one must ask for help in carrying out the required tasks. Paradoxically, only grace can enable one to become fully human, as Christ exemplified humanity in His life and death.

Below: Two latecomers to the vineyard are welcomed by the employer and sent to work. Expecting to receive a lesser wage than the others, they will be surprised to receive a full day's pay—what we would call a living wage.

Wheat and Tares

24 Another parable put he forth unto them, saying, The kingdom of heaven is likened unto a man which sowed good seed in his field:

25 But while men slept, his enemy came and sowed tares among the wheat, and went his way.

26 But when the blade was sprung up, and brought forth fruit, then appeared the tares also.

27 So the servants of the householder came and said unto him, Sir, didst not thou sow good seed in thy field? from whence then hath it tares?

28 He said unto them, An enemy hath done this. The servants said unto him, Wilt thou then that we go and gather them up?

29 But he said, Nay; lest while ye gather up the tares, ye root up also the wheat with them.

30 Let both grow together until the harvest: and in the time of harvest I will say to the reapers, Gather ye together first the tares, and bind them in bundles to burn them: but gather the wheat into my barn.

* * *

36 Then Jesus sent the multitude away, and went into the house: and his disciples came unto him, saying, Declare unto us the parable of the tares of the field.

37 He answered and said unto them, He that soweth the good seed is the Son of man;

38 The field is the world; the good seed are the children of the kingdom; but the tares are the children of the wicked *one*;

39 The enemy that sowed them is the devil; the harvest is the end of the world; and the reapers are the angels.

40 As therefore the tares are gathered and burned in the fire; so shall it be in the end of this world.

41 The Son of man shall send forth his angels, and they

shall gather out of his kingdom all things that offend, and them which do iniquity;

42 And shall cast them into a furnace of fire: there shall be wailing and gnashing of teeth.

43 Then shall the righteous shine forth as the sun in the kingdom of their Father. Who hath ears to hear, let him hear.

—MATTHEW 13:24–30, 36–43

Below: *The theme of a fruitful harvest recurs throughout the Gospels, as here, when the Pharisees reprove Christ's disciples for plucking grain to eat on the Sabbath.*

WORKERS IN THE VINEYARD

1 For the kingdom of heaven is like unto a man *that is* an householder, which went out early in the morning to hire labourers into his vineyard.

2 And when he had agreed with the labourers for a penny a day, he sent them into his vineyard.

3 And he went out about the third hour, and saw others standing idle in the marketplace,

4 And said unto them; Go ye also into the vineyard, and whatsoever is right I will give you. And they went their way.

5 Again he went out about the sixth and ninth hour, and did likewise.

6 And about the eleventh hour he went out, and found others standing idle, and saith unto them, Why stand ye here all the day idle?

7 They say unto him, Because no man hath hired us. He saith unto them, Go ye also into the vineyard; and whatsoever is right, *that* shall ye receive.

8 So when even was come, the lord of the vineyard saith unto his steward, Call the labourers, and give them *their* hire, beginning from the last unto the first.

9 And when they came that *were hired* about the eleventh hour, they received every man a penny.

10 But when the first came, they supposed that they should have received more; and they likewise received every man a penny.

11 And when they had received *it*, they murmured against the goodman of the house,

12 Saying, These last have wrought *but* one hour, and thou hast made them equal unto us, which have borne the burden and heat of the day.

13 But he answered one of them, and said, Friend, I do thee no wrong: didst not thou agree with me for a penny?

14 Take *that thine is*, and go thy way: I will give unto this last, even as unto thee.

15 Is it not lawful for me to do what I will with mine own? Is thine eye evil, because I am good?
16 So the last shall be first, and the first last: for many be called, but few chosen.

—MATTHEW 20:1–16

THE TALENTS

14 For *the kingdom of heaven is* as a man travelling into a far country, *who* called his own servants, and delivered unto them his goods.
15 And unto one he gave five talents, to another two, and to another one; to every man according to his several ability; and straightway took his journey.
16 Then he that had received the five talents went and traded with the same, and made *them* other five talents.
17 And likewise he that *had received* two, he also gained other two.
18 But he that had received one went and digged in the earth, and hid his lord's money.
19 After a long time the lord of those servants cometh, and reckoneth with them.
20 And so he that had received five talents came and brought other five talents, saying, Lord, thou deliveredst unto me five talents: behold, I have gained beside them five talents more.
21 His lord said unto him, Well done, *thou* good and faithful servant: thou hast been faithful over a few things, I will make thee ruler over many things: enter thou into the joy of thy lord.
22 He also that had received two talents came and said, Lord, thou deliveredst unto me two talents: behold, I have gained two other talents beside them.
23 His lord said unto him, Well done, good and faithful servant; thou hast been faithful over a few things, I will

make thee ruler over many things: enter thou into the joy of thy lord.

24 Then he which had received the one talent came and said, Lord, I knew thee that thou art an hard man, reaping where thou hast not sown, and gathering where thou hast not strawed:

25 And I was afraid, and went and hid thy talent in the earth: lo, *there* thou hast *that is* thine.

26 His lord answered and said unto him, *Thou* wicked and slothful servant, thou knewest that I reap where I sowed not, and gather where I have not strawed:

Below: Velázquez's portrait of St. Paul, one of the New Testament's pre-eminent examples of receiving and responding to the call of Christ.

27 Thou oughtest therefore to have put my money to the exchangers, and *then* at my coming I should have received mine own with usury.

28 Take therefore the talent from him, and give *it* unto him which hath ten talents.

29 For unto every one that hath shall be given, and he shall have abundance: but from him that hath not shall be taken away even that which he hath.

30 And cast ye the unprofitable servant into outer darkness: there shall be weeping and gnashing of teeth.

—MATTHEW 25:14–30

THE UNJUST STEWARD

1 And he said also unto his disciples, There was a certain rich man, which had a steward; and the same was accused unto him that he had wasted his goods.

2 And he called him, and said unto him, How is it that I hear this of thee? give an account of thy stewardship; for thou mayest be no longer steward.

3 Then the steward said within himself, What shall I do? for my lord taketh away from me the stewardship: I cannot dig; to beg I am ashamed.

4 I am resolved what to do, that, when I am put out of the stewardship, they may receive me into their houses.

5 So he called every one of his lord's debtors *unto him*, and said unto the first, How much owest thou unto my lord?

6 And he said, An hundred measures of oil. And he said unto him, Take thy bill, and sit down quickly, and write fifty.

7 Then said he to another, And how much owest thou? And he said, An hundred measures of wheat. And he said unto him, Take thy bill, and write fourscore.

8 And the lord commended the unjust steward, because he had done wisely: for the children of this world are in their generation wiser than the children of light.

9 And I say unto you, Make to yourselves friends of the mammon of unrighteousness; that, when ye fail, they may receive you into everlasting habitations.

10 He that is faithful in that which is least is faithful also in much: and he that is unjust in the least is unjust also in much.

11 If therefore ye have not been faithful in the unrighteous mammon, who will commit to your trust the true *riches*?

12 And if ye have not been faithful in that which is another man's, who shall give you that which is your own?

13 No servant can serve two masters: for either he will hate the one, and love the other; or else he will hold to the one, and despise the other. Ye cannot serve God and mammon.

—LUKE 16:1–13

THE LIGHTED CANDLE

21 And he said unto them, Is a candle brought to be put under a bushel, or under a bed? and not to be set on a candlestick?

22 For there is nothing hid, which shall not be manifested; neither was any thing kept secret, but that it should come abroad.

23 If any man have ears to hear, let him hear.

—MARK 4:21–23

Opposite: *Even among His closest friends, Christ found an "unjust steward" in the person of Judas, who held the purse for the Twelve and betrayed his master for money. The engraving of the Last Supper is by Doré.*

THE BODY'S LAMP

33 No man, when he hath lighted a candle, putteth *it* in a secret place, neither under a bushel, but on a candlestick, that they which come in may see the light.

34 The light of the body is the eye: therefore when thine eye is single, thy whole body also is full of light; but when *thine eye* is evil, thy body also *is* full of darkness.

35 Take heed therefore that the light which is in thee be not darkness.

36 If thy whole body therefore *be* full of light, having no part dark, the whole shall be full of light, as when the bright shining of a candle doth give thee light.

—LUKE 11:33–36

Below: *The light of the candle was symbolic of the spiritual illumination imparted by Christ.*

The Rich Fool

Opposite: Christ's mission to feed the hungry in both body and spirit was seen when He multiplied the loaves and the fishes for the multitude.

Below: A nineteenth-century illustrator depicted the Rich Fool counting his money and congratulating himself only hours before his unexpected death.

16 And he spake a parable unto them, saying, The ground of a certain rich man brought forth plentifully:

17 And he thought within himself, saying, What shall I do, because I have no room where to bestow my fruits?

18 And he said, This will I do: I will pull down my barns, and build greater; and there will I bestow all my fruits and my goods.

19 And I will say to my soul, Soul, thou hast much goods laid up for many years; take thine ease, eat, drink, *and* be merry.

20 But God said unto him, *Thou* fool, this night thy soul shall be required of thee: then whose shall those things be, which thou hast provided?

21 So *is* he that layeth up treasure for himself, and is not rich toward God.

—LUKE 12:16–21

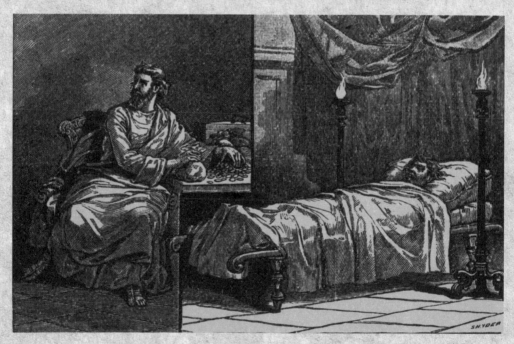

THE TOWER BUILDER AND THE WARRING KING

Below: The virtue of prudence was extolled in the twin parables of the Tower Builder and The Warring King, illustrated here from a medieval Book of Hours.

28 For which of you, intending to build a tower, sitteth not down first, and counteth the cost, whether he have *sufficient* to finish it?

29 Lest haply, after he hath laid the foundation, and is not able to finish *it*, all that behold *it* begin to mock him,

30 Saying, This man began to build, and was not able to finish.

31 Or what king, going to make war against another king, sitteth not down first, and consulteth whether he be able with ten thousand to meet him that cometh against him with twenty thousand?

32 Or else, while the other is yet a great way off, he sendeth an ambassage, and desireth conditions of peace.

—LUKE 14:28–32

On
Spirituality

On Spirituality

Previous page: The Virgin Mary, an exemplar of spirituality, is honored by the Risen Christ in this moving Renaissance work by Titian.

The generosity of God as compared to man overflows in all the parables on spirituality, which encompasses both prayer and grace. In the parable of the Watchful Servants, which is usually interpreted as a warning, the deeper meaning is one of reassurance. Not only are the Watchful Servants commended for staying on the alert for their lord's coming, when he *does* come, he turns the tables by serving them. This recalls the Last Supper, when Christ astonished and humbled his apostles by putting a towel around his waist like a servant and washing their feet in the customary purification ritual. When Peter protested, saying, "Thou shalt never wash my feet," Christ told him: "If I wash thee not, thou hast no part with me" (Jn 13:8). Then Peter assented wholeheartedly, putting aside the conventional notions of the Master/disciple relationship for the new model of a mutual love beyond human comprehension.

The parable of the Great Supper is another illustration of unexpected graciousness. Christ's party-giver, God, is eager to fill his house with guests. First, He invites all the "right" people, but they send their regrets for all the right reasons: business to attend to and so forth. The would-be host is affronted and sends all over town for the local "untouchables"—the blind, the maimed and others whom no respectable householder would think of inviting. Having filled the house with these unlikely guests—whom those on the original guest list wouldn't be caught dead with—the host is entirely content. His total commitment to graciousness is satisfied by giving to those who are shunned by the worldly-wise. He goes so far as to say that "none of those men which were bidden shall taste of my supper." This forecasts the saying found in the parable of the lost sheep: "Joy shall be in heaven over one sinner that repenteth, more than over ninety and nine just persons, which need no repentance."

Another simile on the unseen working of grace is that of the Seed Growing Secretly. The farmer scatters his seed in the field and goes about his business as the crop springs up and flourishes "he knoweth not how." His part is a small one—the real work is done by grace, which will create new life where the smallest sign of willingness is discerned. It operates independently of human notions of justice, self-righteousness, or what must and must not be done to please God. One has already pleased God by the mere fact of being human. It is the act of being itself that gives one an unlimited claim upon the goodness of God as Creator, Redeemer and Sanctifier of all that is.

God's predilection for the least and the lost is emphasized again in Christ's reply to the indignant Pharisees, who demanded: "Why do the disciples of John and of the Pharisees fast, but thy disciples fast not?" As usual, they were seeking to put Him in the wrong because of envy. He had called Levi, one of the despised tax collectors, to follow Him, and ended up dining at Levi's house, which scandalized the self-righteous. Their idea of spirituality was a kind of moral bookkeeping, whereby one fulfilled all the outward prescriptions of the Law. Christ's radical view was that those in most need of grace were the ones for whom He was "the bridegroom." And while He was present among them, they could not fast and had no need to do so. This is another

Opposite: Goya's portrait of St. Peter in fervent prayer with his emblem, the keys to the Kingdom of Heaven.

variation on the theme of the Great Supper, which turned the prevailing notion of grace on its head and made winners of the world's losers.

The parable of the Budding Fig Tree focuses again on the theme of unbounded grace and the goodness to be poured out upon the world through Christ's death and resurrection. The summer foretold by the leafing out of the fig tree "and all the trees" is the unending summer ushered in by the coming of the kingdom of God. It would be manifested fully at the end of time, and Christ's presence in the world was the living sign of that fulfillment: He told His disciples that "Heaven and earth shall pass away: but my words shall not pass away." As the visible, audible Word of God in the world, Christ alone could draw all things to Himself and reconcile them to God.

The Pharisees were offended again when Christ taught that it was not the things a person ate and drank that could defile him, but the things that came out of his mouth at the prompting of an evil heart. As an example, He cited: "murders, adulteries, fornications, thefts, false witness, blasphemies." This ran counter to the whole idea of outward observance as a protection against inner corruption. The contrast was emphasized in the conclusion: "These are the things which defile a man: but to eat with unwashen hands defileth not a man."

Christ's words on inward purity were reinforced by His condemnation of the Pharisees as the blind leading the blind, with the result that "both shall fall into a ditch." This was one of the many occasions on which Christ taught that true spirituality looked always to the free gift of grace, rather than to self-serving ideas of how to compel God's approbation. The Pharisees of this world were censured for multiplying the burdens of religion until they became heavier than people could bear, thus making them feel cut off from God rather than at peace with Him.

One of the best-loved parables is that of the Birds of Heaven and the Lilies of the Field—radical examples of the spirituality of being. The disciples are encouraged to surrender their everyday concerns about food, clothing and other necessities of life and trust in God to provide for them as they seek first the Kingdom. Examples are drawn from nature, showing how the birds are fed and the lilies clothed in brilliant colors without any forethought on their part. The disciples were empowered by grace to take this message fully to heart only after they received the Holy Spirit in the wake of Christ's ascension into heaven. Not until the Acts of the Apostles do we see them consistently following Christ's example and encouragement to "Sell that ye have and give alms; provide yourselves bags which wax not old, a treasure in the heavens that faileth not, where no thief approaches nor moth corrupteth." This parable ends with the telling words that have inspired generations of people in search of true spirituality: "For where your treasure is, there will your heart be also."

THE WATCHFUL SERVANTS

35 Let your loins be girded about, and *your* lights burning;

36 And ye yourselves like unto men that wait for their lord, when he will return from the wedding; that when he cometh and knocketh, they may open unto him immediately.

37 Blessed *are* those servants, whom the lord when he cometh shall find watching: verily I say unto you, that he shall gird himself, and make them to sit down to meat, and will come forth and serve them.

38 And if he shall come in the second watch, or come in the third watch, and find *them* so, blessed are those servants.

39 And this know, that if the goodman of the house had known what hour the thief would come, he would have watched, and not have suffered his house to be broken through.

40 Be ye therefore ready also: for the Son of man cometh at an hour when ye think not.

—LUKE 12:35—40

Right: Two of Christ's watchful servants are surprised and overjoyed when He reveals Himself to them at Emmaus after His resurrection. The luminous painting (1629) is by Velasquez.

THE GREAT SUPPER

16 Then said he unto him, A certain man made a great supper, and bade many:

17 And sent his servant at supper time to say to them that were bidden, Come; for all things are now ready.

18 And they all with one *consent* began to make excuse. The first said unto him, I have bought a piece of ground, and I must needs go and see it: I pray thee have me excused.

19 And another said, I have bought five yoke of oxen, and I go to prove them: I pray thee have me excused.

20 And another said, I have married a wife, and therefore I cannot come.

21 So that servant came, and shewed his lord these things. Then the master of the house being angry said to his servant, Go out quickly into the streets and lanes of the city, and bring in hither the poor, and the maimed, and the halt, and the blind.

22 And the servant said, Lord, it is done as thou hast commanded, and yet there is room.

23 And the lord said unto the servant, Go out into the highways and hedges, and compel *them* to come in, that my house may be filled.

24 For I say unto you, That none of those men which were bidden shall taste of my supper.

—LUKE 14:16–24

Below: The people invited to the Great Supper, depicted here as sheep shearers from a medieval Book of Hours, were too busy with their everyday concerns to respond.

THE SEED GROWING SECRETLY

Below: The Incarnation, when the Christ Child was conceived of the Virgin Mary by the Holy Spirit, was a profound example of the Seed Growing Secretly. This Renaissance painting of the event is by Tintoretto (1583).

26 And he said, So is the kingdom of God, as if a man should cast seed into the ground;

27 And should sleep, and rise night and day, and the seed should spring and grow up, he knoweth not how.

28 For the earth bringeth forth fruit of herself; first the blade, then the ear, after that the full corn in the ear.

29 But when the fruit is brought forth, immediately he putteth in the sickle, because the harvest is come.

—MARK 4:26–29

PRAYER AND FASTING

14 And as he passed by, he saw Levi the *son* of Alphaeus sitting at the receipt of custom, and said unto him, Follow me. And he arose and followed him.

15 And it came to pass, that, as Jesus sat at meat in his house, many publicans and sinners sat also together with Jesus and his disciples: for there were many, and they followed him.

16 And when the scribes and Pharisees saw him eat with publicans and sinners, they said unto his disciples, How is it that he eateth and drinketh with publicans and sinners?

17 When Jesus heard *it*, he saith unto them, They that are whole have no need of the physician, but they that are sick: I came not to call the righteous, but sinners to repentance.

18 And the disciples of John and of the Pharisees used to fast: and they come and say unto him, Why do the disciples of John and of the Pharisees fast, but thy disciples fast not?

19 And Jesus said unto them, Can the children of the bridechamber fast, while the bridegroom is with them? as long as they have the bridegroom with them, they cannot fast.

20 But the days will come, when the bridegroom shall be taken away from them, and then shall they fast in those days.

—MARK 2:14–20

Below: *St. John the Evangelist, by Titian, followed Christ's example of prayer, fasting and almsgiving throughout his long lifetime. He was the only apostle who did not die a martyr's death.*

THE BUDDING FIG TREE

29 And he spake to them a parable; Behold the fig tree, and all the trees;

30 When they now shoot forth, ye see and know of your own selves that summer is now nigh at hand.

31 So likewise ye, when ye see these things come to pass, know ye that the kingdom of God is nigh at hand.

32 Verily I say unto you, This generation shall not pass away, till all be fulfilled.

33 Heaven and earth shall pass away: but my words shall not pass away.

—LUKE 21:29–33

ON INWARD PURITY

10 And he called the multitude, and said unto them, Hear, and understand:

11 Not that which goeth into the mouth defileth a man; but that which cometh out of the mouth, this defileth a man.

12 Then came his disciples, and said unto him, Knowest thou that the Pharisees were offended, after they heard this saying?

13 But he answered and said, Every plant, which my heavenly Father hath not planted, shall be rooted up.

14 Let them alone: they be blind leaders of the blind. And if the blind lead the blind, both shall fall into the ditch.

15 Then answered Peter and said unto him, Declare unto us this parable.

16 And Jesus said, Are ye also yet without understanding?

17 Do not ye yet understand, that whatsoever entereth in at the mouth goeth into the belly, and is cast out into the draught?

18 But those things which proceed out of the mouth come forth from the heart; and they defile the man.

19 For out of the heart proceed evil thoughts, murders, adulteries, fornications, thefts, false witness, blasphemies:

20 These are the *things* which defile a man: but to eat with unwashen hands defileth not a man.

—MATTHEW 15:10–20

Left: *Christ is baptized by his cousin John, "the voice of one crying in the wilderness," in this engraving by Doré. The rite signified inward purity and revealed Christ as the promised Messiah.*

THE BIRDS OF HEAVEN AND THE LILIES OF THE FIELD

22 And he said unto his disciples, Therefore I say unto you, Take no thought for your life, what ye shall eat; neither for the body, what ye shall put on.

23 The life is more than meat, and the body *is more* than raiment.

24 Consider the ravens: for they neither sow nor reap; which neither have storehouse nor barn; and God feedeth them: how much more are ye better than the fowls?

25 And which of you with taking thought can add to his stature one cubit?

26 If ye then be not able to do that thing which is least, why take ye thought for the rest?

27 Consider the lilies how they grow: they toil not, they spin not; and yet I say unto you, that Solomon in all his glory was not arrayed like one of these.

28 If then God so clothe the grass, which is to day in the field, and to morrow is cast into the oven; how much more *will he clothe you*, O ye of little faith?

29 And seek not ye what ye shall eat, or what ye shall drink, neither be ye of doubtful mind.

30 For all these things do the nations of the world seek after: and your Father knoweth that ye have need of these things.

31 But rather seek ye the kingdom of God; and all these things shall be added unto you.

—LUKE 12:22–31

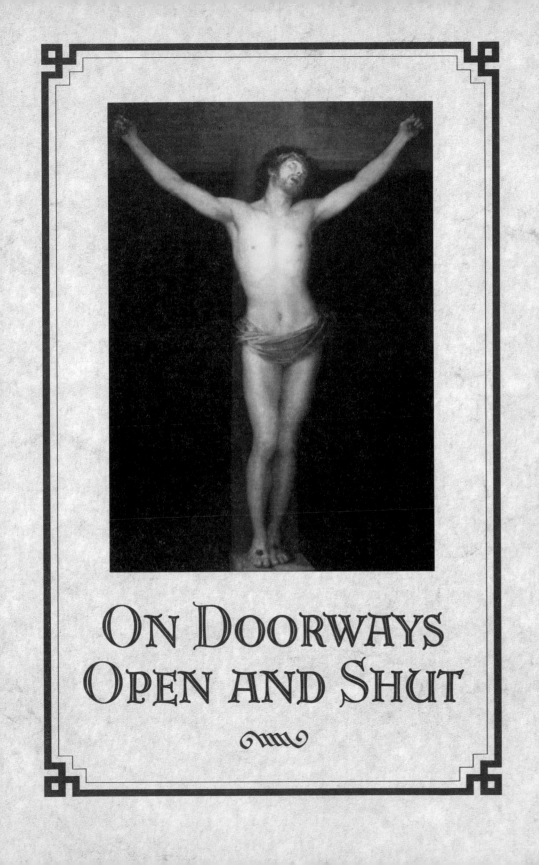

On Doorways
Open and Shut

On Doorways
Open and Shut

Previous page: Goya's painting of the crucified Christ, whose death reopened the doors of eternal life to humankind.

The old order and the new are contrasted in a number of parables that speak of doorways, gates and guardians of these openings. In the parable of the Divided Realm, Christ confounded those critics who accused Him of doing good works through sorcery rather than by the power of God. He pointed out that the kingdom of Satan (the Adversary) was inherently divided against itself and would ultimately fail. It was powerless against the Kingdom of God, which worked toward healing and happiness, not self-destruction. This statement was reinforced by the story of the Strong Man Bound—another type of the evil powers that Christ had come to overthrow and dispossess. Identifying Himself with the Suffering Servant prophesied by Isaiah, He proclaimed Himself the victor who would overcome the strong and redistribute their goods ("spoils") to the needy. The Jews were awaiting the time predicted in the words of the Assumption of Moses: "His Kingdom shall appear throughout all His creation; And Satan shall be no more; And sorrow shall depart with him." In these parables, Christ announced the arrival of the promised Kingdom through His power to overcome all evil.

Luke placed the parable of the Defendant with a series of warnings about the coming crisis of choice between old and new. These warnings are just as applicable today, in the face of world hunger, overpopulation and a growing schism between the rich and the rest of us. Reflective people of many faiths see the potential for widespread breakdowns of the social order under these stresses. However, the solution does not lie in violence, but in seeking reconciliation before estrangement becomes total. The counsel to agree with one's adversary on the way to the magistrate has wide-ranging implications. Willingness to keep open the door to mutual understanding, whether between persons or nations, builds peace rather than conflict.

The parable of the Closed Door (also called the Narrow Gate) is often interpreted as a warning, but it is, in fact, an invitation to accept grace, the unexpected gift beyond our hopes. Christ is the "master of the house" who "is risen up" to admit everyone who has embraced His example of unconditional love. Those who knock at the door demanding entrance but are left standing outside are like the guest who came to the Wedding Feast without the right clothing. They have not fully understood that they must put off the old grasping, selfish ways and put on what St. Paul called "the armour of light"—willingness to follow Christ's example of selfless love and trust in God. In this parable, Christ emphasizes again that the kingdom will be filled from the four corners of the earth and that "there be last which shall be first and there are first which shall be last."

In the parable of the Doorkeeper, watchfulness is the quality that admits "the master" and wins his approbation. Grace may come at any time: "at even [evening], or at midnight, or at the cockcrowing, or in the morning." The doorkeeper who is vigilant will not lose any opportunity to admit life-giving grace, whereas the one who is sleeping

Below: A youthful St. John the Baptist in the wilderness, painted by Raphael, assumes his role as the herald of Christ's coming into the world.

misses the chance to experience spiritual growth through openness to new ideas, new courage and the "daily bread" of God's compassionate support.

"How much more" is the theme of the Son's Request, which compares God to a conscientious human father who answers a child's request for food. Christ shocks his listeners into awareness when He asks: "What man is there of you, whom if his son ask bread, will give him a stone? Or if he ask a fish, will he give him a serpent?" He points out that the goodness of God is far beyond that of human beings, no matter how well-intentioned, and that perseverance in prayer will always be rewarded in God's own time: "For every one that asketh receiveth; and he that seeketh findeth; and to him that knocketh it shall be opened."

In ancient Middle Eastern weddings, the bridegroom was the focus of attention rather than the bride. In the parable of the Wise and Foolish Virgins, Christ is the bridegroom. All the bride's friends gather by night to await his arrival and attend him to the ceremony, but he is delayed and half the girls fall asleep and let their lamps go out. They beg the others for oil to rekindle their lamps, but are refused and hurry off to find a store that may still be open. Meanwhile, the whole bridal party enters the festive house and shuts the door. Failure to pay attention to what they were doing caused them to miss their opportunity, like the drowsy porter who fell asleep while awaiting his master's return from a journey. The interpretation of this parable as one of the Parousia, or Second Coming, did not arise until the first century AD, when the early Christian Church began to describe itself as the Bride of Christ.

The much-loved parable of the Good Shepherd was told shortly before Christ's passion and death. It sums up his ministry in the moving image of the shepherd who lays down his life for his sheep. When Christ described Himself as "the door of the sheep," His meaning was clear to the country people of Palestine. It was customary for the shepherd to gather his flock every evening and to pen them up in a rude enclosure. He slept at the entrance, guarding the flock with his own body. The sheep would not step over his sleeping form any more than they would answer the call of another shepherd ("the hireling"). If a wolf or other predator tried to get in, the shepherd would defend the flock with his life, while the hireling fled. In this parable, Christ referred to false prophets and other imposters as thieves and robbers, "but the sheep did not hear them...for they know not the voice of strangers."

This parable is so important that it is repeated immediately and expanded upon in the words: "I am the good shepherd: the good shepherd giveth his life for the sheep. [I] know my sheep, and am known of mine." The universality of Christ's mission is seen in the concluding verse: "Other sheep I have, which are not of this fold: them also I must bring, and they shall hear my voice; and there shall be one fold, and one shepherd." The theme of ultimate unity and peace is the consoling note struck by this parable as Christ "set his face toward Jerusalem" to lay down His life and take it up again.

Below: *Christ presides over the Last Supper in a Renaissance painting by Titian, which captures the intimacy and homeliness of His relationship with His followers.*

THE DIVIDED REALM AND THE STRONG MAN BOUND

Below: *Christ as healer personifies the strength that overcomes the Divided Realm of evil in this engraving by Doré.*

17 But he, knowing their thoughts, said unto them, Every kingdom divided against itself is brought to desolation; and a house *divided* against a house falleth.

18 If Satan also be divided against himself, how shall his kingdom stand? because ye say that I cast out devils through Beelzebub.

19 And if I by Beelzebub cast out devils, by whom do your sons cast *them* out? therefore shall they be your judges.

20 But if I with the finger of God cast out devils, no doubt the kingdom of God is come upon you.

21 When a strong man armed keepeth his palace, his goods are in peace:

22 But when a stronger than he shall come upon him, and overcome him, he taketh from him all his armour wherein he trusted, and divideth his spoils.

—LUKE 11:17—22

THE DEFENDANT

58 When thou goest with thine adversary to the magistrate, *as thou art* in the way, give diligence that thou mayest be delivered from him; lest he hale thee to the judge, and the judge deliver thee to the officer, and the officer cast thee into prison.

59 I tell thee, thou shalt not depart thence, till thou hast paid the very last mite.

—LUKE 12:58–59

Below: *Surmounted by the Greek letters Alpha and Omega (the beginning and the end), the Risen Christ is seated in judgement with the Holy Trinity, by Raphael.*

THE CLOSED DOOR

Opposite: The Gates of Hell, sculpted by Rodin, were a frequent motif in medieval and Renaissance art.

Below: Roger van der Weyden's portrayal of Christ on the Cross.

24 Strive to enter in at the strait gate: for many, I say unto you, will seek to enter in, and shall not be able.

25 When once the master of the house is risen up, and hath shut to the door, and ye begin to stand wihout, and to knock at the door, saying, Lord, Lord, open unto us; and he shall answer and say unto you, I know you not whence ye are:

26 Then shall ye begin to say, We have eaten and drunk in thy presence, and thou hast taught in our streets.

27 But he shall say, I tell you, I know not when ye are; depart from me, all ye workers of iniquity.

28 There shall be weeping and gnashing of teeth, when ye shall see Abraham, and Isaac, and Jacob, and all the prophets, in the kingdom of God, and you *yourselves* thrust out.

29 And they shall come from the east, and *from* the west, and from the north, and *from* the south, and shall sit down in the kingdom of God.

30 And, behold, there are last which shall be first, and there are first which shall be last.

—LUKE 13:24–30

THE SON'S REQUEST

9   Or what man is there of you, whom if his son ask bread, will he give him a stone?

10   Or if he ask a fish, will he give him a serpent?

11   If ye then, being evil, know how to give good gifts unto your children, how much more shall your Father which is in heaven give good things to them that ask him?

12   Therefore all things whatsoever ye would that men should do to you, do ye even so to them: for this is the law and the prophets.

—MATTHEW 7:9–12

Below: Renoir's painting of his child at play (1905) recalls the theme of parental love addressed in the parable of the Son's Request.

THE WISE AND FOOLISH VIRGINS

1   Then shall the kingdom of heaven be likened unto ten virgins, which took their lamps, and went forth to meet the bridegroom.

2   And five of them were wise, and five *were* foolish.

3   They that were foolish took their lamps, and took no oil with them:

4   But the wise took oil in their vessels with their lamps.

5   While the bridegroom tarried, they all slumberedand slept.

6   And at midnight there was a cry made, Behold, the bridegroom cometh; go ye out to meet him.

7   Then all those virgins arose, and trimmed their lamps.

8   And the foolish said unto the wise, Give us of your oil; for our lamps are gone out.

9   But the wise answered, saying, *Not so*; lest there be not enough for us and you: but go ye rather to them that sell, and buy for yourselves.

10 And while they went to buy, the bridegroom came; and they that were ready went in with him to the marriage: and the door was shut.

11 Afterward came also the other virgins, saying, Lord, Lord, open to us.

12 But he answered and said, Verily I say unto you, I know you not.

13 Watch therefore, for ye know neither the day nor the hour wherein the Son of man cometh.

Above: *A nineteenth-century illustration of the Wise and Foolish Virgins awaiting the coming of the bridegroom: those who fell asleep and let their lamps go out were barred from the wedding feast.*

—MATTHEW 25:1–13

THE GOOD SHEPHERD

1   Verily, verily, I say unto you, He that entereth not by the door into the sheepfold, but climbeth up some other way, the same is a thief and a robber.

2   But he that entereth in by the door is the shepherd of the sheep.

3   To him the porter openeth; and the sheep hear his voice: and he calleth his own sheep by name, and leadeth them out.

4   And when he putteth forth his own sheep, he goeth before them, and the sheep follow him: for they know his voice.

5   And a stranger will they not follow, but will flee from him: for they know not the voice of strangers.

6   This parable spake Jesus unto them: but they understood not what things they were which he spake unto them.

7   Then said Jesus unto them again, Verily, verily, I say unto you, I am the door of the sheep.

8   All that ever came before me are thieves and robbers: but the sheep did not hear them.

9   I am the door: by me if any man enter in, he shall be saved, and shall go in and out, and find pasture.

10 The thief cometh not, but for to steal, and to kill, and to destroy: I am come that they might have life, and that they might have *it* more abundantly.

* * *

13 The hireling fleeth, because he is an hireling, and careth not for the sheep.

14 I am the good shepherd, and know my *sheep*, and am known of mine.

15 As the Father knoweth me, even so know I the Father: and I lay down my life for the sheep.

16 And other sheep I have, which are not of this fold: them also I must bring, and they shall hear my voice; and there shall be one fold, *and* one shepherd.

—JOHN 10:1–16

Index of Parables

Page numbers in *italics* refer to illustrations.